Total Devastation

My Story

Tara Herring

TOTAL DEVASTATION:
MY STORY

Copyright Tara Herring, 2020

ISBN 978-0-578-81632-6

Manufactured in the United States of America
First printing December 2020

Disclosure: I am not telling anyone what to do or say. I am not telling anyone how they should deal with situations in life. I am not telling anyone how to live. I am not telling anyone what is right or wrong. I am expressing my views and what I believe by telling my story.

My mother always complained about how my father always got the credit for everything throughout life. This is dedicated to my mother for always being there for me with unconditional love and loving me just as I am. Throughout life when everyone turned their back on me my mother was always there. When I was weak, she was strong. Now when she is weak, I am strong for her. No one can take our close bond we have away from us even though it may look like it from the outside. I have been so blessed to have a mother like her.

This book might not be the best in the world, but it takes negative power away and replaces it with positive. It puts mine and my mother's relationship back to what it was if not better. You might be wondering why I am writing a book instead of just telling her. My lifetime hired mentor her name is Roxy. Roxy had her put a restraining order on me against her. My mother is a victim caught between Roxy and me fighting. This is all I can do at this point. My mother is eighty-four, and I am so afraid of her passing away with things as they are now. I am not going to court because I don't want mine and my mother's last memories to be in a courthouse. That is what Roxy wants. Roxy wants my mother to have a nervous breakdown like she did when I was fourteen. I refuse to give Roxy what she wants. I have no other choice than to write this book.

My entire life I have been able to just walk away from anything and start over with no problem. I am a single, forty-eight-year-old woman with three grown kids, and for some reason I can't just walk away this time. I asked my higher power (I am spiritual), "Can you please just take me now, I cannot take anymore." He keeps letting me live. I could not be that lucky. Even though I don't believe in luck. I have been to the doctor and even though I have battled with depression in the past I am not depressed. I am broken beyond repair. Total devastation. It is not only my life it is the entire world and there is nothing I can do except tell my story.

My mother raised me to challenge my brain every day. I have used this throughout life. When a problem happened, she would tell me to ask myself why, to detach from the world and look at myself and my patterns, then to also look at other people's patterns. That is when you can connect the dots and make changes in your life. If your intentions are good you have nothing to worry about. Although we are all human and life happens. Bad things always happen to everyone. That is just life. You must learn how to roll with the punches and always keep love in your heart. My father said, "Don't just sit there and pray, do the footwork." Even though I know throughout life I have always had the best intentions nothing ever seems to work out the way I had hoped. It seems like I am always wrong no matter what. How can life be so hard for someone with a good heart and good intentions? It makes life very frustrating if I surround myself with toxic people. I will do what makes me happy and don't care much about material things. Don't get me wrong I like nice things, but I would much rather shop at a secondhand store. If I am happy, my children will be happy. I am an introvert. I much rather be by myself. Doing silly things just to make someone smile makes me happy. If they think I am crazy and smile I am ok with that. I believe people take life way to serous all the time. I do realize that there is situation that you should take seriously but what about the rest of the time? Why be so serous all the time? I laugh at myself all the time and it feels good. I will drive jam my music and dance in my car. It makes me feel happy. I am high off life. People will laugh and smile at me. It feels good to see someone in the car beside me smile and laugh. It is something about laughter that fills your body up with positive energy. It is good for the soul. I know I am different but that is not a bad thing. Why can't you just let people be who they are instead of trying to make them the same as you are. If people were all the same do you know how boring life would be? What makes me different makes me beautiful. It also makes it harder. I always seem to come across as sounding better than. I am not better than I am just different. I understand everyone in life has seemed to put a label on me because it is what they struggle with. I understand the struggles with an alcoholic, and I can empathize with that. If I was one, I would say I was. You should not push what works for you does not work for everybody. What applies to you doesn't apply with everyone. That does not always mean someone is in denial. It could simply mean that you cannot put that label on everyone who drinks alcohol. I don't fit in anywhere. I am fully aware of that. I am a deep thinker that is all that is wrong with me. I can see through your bullshit and no one likes it. I am quiet. I lost a boyfriend in high school because he said I didn't talk. I sit back and observe people. I read your body language and I can feel your aura. I don't care for small talk. I always remember the first thing said to me when something traumatic happens in life because stories change after that. I never believe what people say or their actions. What I firmly believe in is patterns. I also know if you see at pattern in your life you don't like you change it. I also believe I should not have to think this hard right now I should be with my mother.

I was born in Virginia to two loving parents. I am an only child. They tried a long time to have me. After sixteen years of trying to conceive a child, I was finally born in June 1972. At age two years old I moved with my parents to Australia where I resided for two years. Then we moved back to the same house in Virginia where I grew up. My school years were great. My friends were awesome.

Still, I could tell even then I didn't fit in. It was not them it was me. I was always the quiet one at the slumber parties. Everyone's conver-sation between each other just seemed so easy. It just flowed out of their mouths so easily. I wished I could be more like that. I didn't know why it was so hard for me to communicate with others. I am highly intelligent in my thinking. If you looked at my grades or spelling, you wouldn't be able to tell. I graduated high school with a four-month-old daughter on my hip and straight C's as my final grades.

During grade school, my mom read to me because everyone seemed to be able to read so much faster. My mother was able to be a stay-at-home mother. My father was the breadwinner. My mother was able to have her dream job as a stay-at-home mother because of my father. My father did that for her because he loved her. He made enough money. He didn't have to do that but he did. When I was in grade school, though, my mother wanted to work so she could have her own money. When I was old enough, she got a job driving a school bus. After a few weeks, I begged her to stop working because I missed her after school. My mother quit her job so she could be there when I got home from school. That was something she did not have to do. She made a sacrifice for her child. That too often goes unnoticed and not appreciated.

During fifth grade, a sixth grader named Trudy yelled in front of the whole class that I stole her quarter. Everyone looked at me and people started yelling things at me. I did not take her quarter; if I wanted a quarter, my mom would give me a dollar. From that moment on, my life at school changed. It was not anyone except for Trudy. Trudy was so much bigger than me and so mean. She would wait for me at the end of the hallway after school. I was always by myself, and I never told anyone. Trudy would corner me and scream at me. A few times, she kicked my ass. I would go home crying to my mother. I would never tell her because I knew she would go to the school and tell them. I knew it would only make it worse on me with Trudy at school. My mother would hold me as I cried, and I begged her not to go to the school. The following year, Trudy had gone to middle school and I went into sixth grade, which is still elementary school. What it did was split us up, and I felt so free. I felt as I had a new beginning. That year was so awesome with my school friends. My friends were great. They liked me just the way I was. I never did get asked to the sixth grade dance, but they all did. I was ok with that. It just wasn't for me. I am shy, so I am not easy to talk to. I knew it was me.

I was in softball from age seven to twelve with my father as the coach. When I entered middle school, my softball team had changed. My father was the coach and there was another father as a coach. That other coach was Trudy's father. Now Trudy is one of my softball team members. I felt safe because my father was there. I never told my father about Trudy bulling me. I thought I would be ok because he was a coach. I loved softball. It was my passion. At age twelve, I received an award for the highest batting average over the entire Vienna Virginia League. I could not believe it. I was feeling so good about that. My parents were proud of me. They were there when I received the award. They ended up framing it for me along with the team picture. I still have that today. What happened after that is Trudy started telling all the girls on the league that I was a bully. They all stopped talking to me and started talking about me. It crushed me, and I didn't tell anyone. I started cutting myself to release all the pain inside from Trudy bullying me. It helped but only for a little while. I was laying on the floor watching television with my mother and my sleeve came down. I had carved a cross in my arm. My mother was so upset and crying. I started running away never to return. This had nothing to do with my mother or father. It was because of all the bullying and not knowing how to talk about it. It was me not my mother or father. It was me.

Even though my parents were there to support me with all these challenges I had faced, it wasn't enough. The pain inside was unbearable. The last time I ran away, I jumped out of my bedroom window two stories high. I landed on my feet, and my knee hit my eye. I had a huge black eye. The neighbor in the back saw me, and I took off never to return. I was gone a long time. My mother had a nervous breakdown and ended up in the hospital. My mother's health was getting worse because I was gone, and she didn't know where I was. She didn't know if she would get that phone call saying I was dead. My mother told me that is the only time she has ever seen my father cry. If you knew him, he doesn't cry. I was breaking the law all the time, so I was eventually picked up by the police and sent to the detention center. Looking at me being locked up for a few years, my parents asked if they could send me to a treatment facility instead so I could receive counseling. The judge agreed and sent me there for a year. I was never diagnosed with a mental illness or a drug/alcohol problem. The gift I was given was a very close relationship with my mother and father. We learned how to communicate, and I felt close to both of them. Do you know I would thank both of them throughout my life for never giving up on me. I had ten months of intense therapy by myself with a counselor. Then had it also with my parents. I was done in ten months instead of a year. Even though I wanted to stay, my conselor made me go home. I had just gotten comfortable.

When I got home, I felt so good. I had a new start on life again, a new beginning. I was in high school and met so many awesome people. A couple of them I still talk to, and they helped me through that difficult time with their positive words. Margret and Kate, I hope you both know how much you mean to me. You helped me in ways that my words can't even say. You didn't even say much, but what you said to me gave me more strength than you realize.

At age fifteen, I met my high school sweetheart Kyle. He took me camping for the first time. It was a wonderful experience. The conversation just flowed like no other. The laughter we shared was such a good feeling. He is such a beautiful man, good-hearted and strong. We went to Luray Caverns, and it was breathtaking. The colors and the formations of the stone were amazing. It was nothing I had ever seen before. Another time we drove Skyline Drive. The beauty of the mountains. The fall is the best time. When you drive, you see so many different colors from the leaves changing. Tranquility. Along the drive you feel so relaxed and free. It is the best feeling in the world.

I ended up getting pregnant. I was sixteen and so excited. I continued to go to high school. None of my friends judged me; they were happy for me.

I had my daughter at seventeen, a beautiful baby girl. We were so happy. I took six weeks off school to care for my daughter. I was able to go back to high school after that because of my mother. My mother allowed me to graduate from high school by watching my daughter for me while I went to school. She did not have to do that, but she did. I was able to graduate with my four-month daughter on my hip because of my mother. My mother made sacrifices for me that I appreciate and thank her every day for. I have thanked her throughout my lifetime. I always make sure she knows I appreciate her and love her.

Kyle and I were just too young and ended up going separate ways even though we loved each other. He passed away when I was going through a year of chemotherapy and then radiation for breast cancer in 2009. Some say it was suicide by a gunshot to the head. Some say it was drugs or a fight. I know what it was. A thought is just a thought unless we act to it. Everyone has fucked-up thoughts. Some just hide there's better than others. I always remember that first phone call and nothing after that. He had just bought a new gun. It had a hair trigger, and he was not use to the gun. Even though he has said it his entire life that when things were going wrong "I want to die" that doesn't mean he wanted to die. It is calling putting a thought into action. That is why you always should detach from everyone and everything when things go wrong in life. You do that so you can get your thoughts together and gain new perspective. I am not telling anyone to do anything. I am just telling my story and expressing my views. I am hoping to help someone who felt as lonely and misunderstood as I did. I have chosen to never owing a gun and never will. It is not that I fear my thoughts because my thoughts are of love not hate. It is because it was an accident, and no one sees that but me. I am ok with that and have dealt with it. That is their battle not mine. In life, you pick your battles. If you think any different that battle is from within you not me.

I ended up getting my dream job of repairing computers. Full-time college just seemed like a waste of money to me. I could get the same schooling with hands-on-training with a trade school. It wouldn't be as long either. I could graduate in two years of full-time school. I was so excited. Next, I had to do some research to see the overall demand for this job. I needed to know if this is something that was worth my time. Meaning is it going to benefit me throughout life. Everything I read made me feel confident about the trade school I picked. My mother allowed me to fulfill my dream as a hardware computer technician with an equal to a two-year degree in electronics. My mother once again watched my daughter while I went to that technical school for two years full-time. My mother is why I graduated.

After graduating, I ended up landing a job repairing computers board level. This is when I met my next baby daddy, Ryan. After a short time, we moved into a place together along with my three-year-old daughter. It was amazing. I ended up finding a job in D.C. as a Network LAN/WAN Administrator. My career was going wonderful. I went from $10 an hour to $45,000 a year. I ended up getting pregnant, and had a baby boy we named Ryan Junior. I named him after his father. I always wished we could have stayed together. I wanted to get married, but he could not commit. Even though I loved him, I had to move out and let him go. I was wanting to grow in the relationship, and he wanted to stay where he was at.

He just passed in the last two years. I have had a difficult time with him being gone. He was a wonderful father to both of my children. Ryan was always so much fun to be around. Some say he overdosed on heroin. Some say it was organ failure. They pulled the plug on him before our son was notified. He passed with never being married and not having a power of attorney or will in Virginia. All the responsibility falls on the oldest child with no power of attorney or will. It was the worst experience I have ever been through. My daughter and son and I had to deal with all of this. I can't even come to the fact he is gone let alone sympathized with how my children are feeling. You see that my middle son is his son. He always thought of my daughter as his own. He was a wonderful father to both. Nothing can take that. Nothing. In the end, it is not what others say or believe. All the matters are that you know the facts. You know that shit happens in life and you deal with it the best you can. I told my children that I thought he over dosed and it was his fault. They both started screaming at me saying I was drunk. I was not drinking or drunk. They pulled over and got out to call a ride because I rented that van. I called the police and asked them to give me a breathalyzer. It was negative. I asked the police officer "Could you please tell my two adult children the negative results and I will leave." He kindly said "Yes," and I left. I cried and prayed to my higher power for ten hours driving home by myself. The pain was unbearable. I don't want to let Ryan go. I love him deeply. I know I must now and will do it the way I see is best for me when the time is right.

Now onto my third baby's daddy, Jerald. I have three adult children with three different fathers. I had met a man in so-called corporate America. He was amazing, and he rode a motorcycle just like my father did. We moved in together, and that is the time I saw my first meteor shower with him. I will never forget it. The sky was beautiful. We made $100,000 a year together. I went on business trips, and I was debt free. Yes, I was making $60,000 a year as a Network LAN/WAN Administrator in Washington, D.C. My commute in the morning was two hours then three hours to arrive home from work. I had to drop and pickup my children to a daycare center. The daycare center allowed me to go to work at my dream job. It was my dream job, and my parents were proud of me. When I reflect on my life, this was the best time of my entire life. What happened is I let Roxy back into my life with just one phone conversation. Even though I know it was her in the end, I can only blame myself. I let her persuade my decision by her negative words. Then I believed all the false promises she made me. What happened is he went to the strip club and never came home. I called her crying. Wrong move on my part. Her positive words would only benefit her not me. Roxy always does things that will benefit only her in the end. I then decided to uproot my two children and leave my dream job, all in one weekend. I moved into my parents' house without them knowing until I showed up on their doorstep. That is a decision I would regret for the rest of my life. As much as I wanted to blame her, I can't. When you decide in life what you are going to do, the only person who pays for a bad decision is you. In the end you are the one who must look yourself in the mirror and deal with it all. You just need to remember that people with bad intentions can be the ones that you love the most and are socially accepted.

What happened to me and his sons' father is I had fallen in love with someone else named Billy Joe. I saw Billy Joe as my soulmate. Even though we have both gone separate ways, and we are both happy and don't talk, he always will be my soul mate. We went to Stone Mountain, and it was the best time I had in a long time. We went to my first bluegrass festival together. We danced and laughed; it felt so good being with him. I do believe you can have a soul mate and not be physically together. It is about the passion we shared with each other. The happiness he brought to my heart that I will always remember. When I reflected on my entire life, it was then I realized why I kept my last boyfriend around. He looked just like Billy Joe. I had subconsciously picked a man that look just like Billy Joe. Once I realized this, I had to acknowledge it, deal with it the best I knew how, then let it go. I then could move forward. I have let it go, and I am moving forward. I will always love you, Billy Joe ,even though I know I will never see you again.

After we separated, I got an apartment with my three kids by myself. Life was going so well, and I was happy. My daughter had given birth to my handsome grandson, Lewis. I was able to be in the room while she delivered him. It was amazing. I am a single mother. I had a three-bedroom apartment with two boys in one room and my daughter and grandson in the other room. I had found a job at a university that I loved. They were getting ready to hire me. I had worked hard for six months in the English Department through a temp agency – always on time, never missed a day of work and the staff loved me.

Then I went to the doctor because I had a lump. I had had the lump for six months. I was waiting until I got insurance from this job. It got bigger and harder, and something told me I should go to the doctors now. I went to a free clinic. They had me go to another doctor to have it biopsied. I never told anyone and went alone. I was thinking so positive that I could never imagine it could be cancer. Well it was breast cancer the lump was huge, and it was aggressive. It had spread into my body because I waited too long to go to the doctors. I had to tell the university. I did not want to lie to them just to get hired. I told my boss and they laid me off because I would not be able to do the duties while going through chemotherapy and radiation. Even though I understood why they laid me off it broke my heart losing my job. I was able to keep my apartment by myself with my three children and grandson. I was also able to keep my car, but I had no extra money for anything. I had everything I needed. My mother was there for me. If I needed anything all I had to do was call her. I never needed any material things all I needed was to hear her sweet voice on the phone and I felt better. The positive I was able to pull out of having cancer was it gave me a new outlook on life. I found happiness in the simple things in life.

After one of my chemotherapy sessions, I received a phone call from my mother that Kyle had passed. In the end, does it matter how someone dies? No, it doesn't because once they are gone, they are gone and there is nothing you can do. My daughter, Sarah, was a teenager and had a job at the mall. I had to call the owner and tell them what happened and that I would talk to her after work. It was one of the hardest conversations I have with my daughter. I drove Sarah and my grandson Lewis eight hours and got a hotel room where he lived. I was still going through chemotherapy, so I had to reschedule my next chemotherapy appointment. They pushed it back a month so I would have time to take Sarah and Lewis to the funeral. At the funeral, Sarah asked why there wasn't an open casket. I looked at her with tears rolling down my face and said nothing. I couldn't do it. I couldn't tell her. I will never forget on the way home Lewis just started laughing so hard and wouldn't stop. Sarah and I both looked at each other with a concerned look wondering what was wrong with him. He would not stop laughing it finally made us both laugh so hard our stomachs hurt. It was a good feeling at a bad time. Laughter is the best medicine in life.

I ended up completing my cancer treatment in 2011 after a year and a half. Did you know you get to ring the bell when you are done? It is an awesome feeling to ring that bell. The bell also gives others that are still going through chemotherapy hope. I also received an award after my radiation was done. It says I completed radiation and my name. That also made me feel good. Thank you for letting me ring the bell and giving me an award.

I tried so hard to find a job, and my unemployment was close to running out. I had to move back in with my parents because I couldn't find a job fast enough. My three kids, grandson and I moved in with my parents. They welcomed us with open arms and love. They did not have to do that, but they did. My mother was there for me again. I continued looking for a job with a positive attitude. I was so excited with the thought of going back to work again. I didn't care where it was just if I was working. I had met my ex-husband online at a dating website. We connected, and it was wonderful. I had my mammogram appointment that I went to. They found a lump on my other breast. Yes, I still have my breast, something I later would regret forever. I went for another biopsy, and it was breast cancer again. It was aggressive, too, which is not common for the second time. I screamed, "No not again! Why me, why me?" Well, why not me? I embraced it. I got married and moved far away from Roxy. We went from poor going through chemotherapy to own-ing my first home. We both had new cars and were very happy.

Years later, I let one toxic person back into my life, Roxy. With one text from Roxy, out of the blue of negative things about my ex-husband that I never said. I don't hide my phone, so of course he read it. With that one text, she planted a negative seed into my husband's mind on purpose. It was a planned attack on my happiness. In a few years, I lost everyone I loved. Roxy even had me pulled over by the police on three different occasions and was asked off-the-wall questions. I was never given a ticket or arrested any of these times. Roxy has put a hit out on me. Roxy told the police I am armed and dangerous. I am happy, high on life and do not have a gun. Roxy, the police aren't buying your story. Roxy, abort your mission of hate. Your battle is not with me. It is with yourself.

I knew I was going into a battlefield to protect my mother. I was prepared for anything. Or at least that is what I thought. Within a six-month period of being around Roxy I had been to the emergency room three times. The first time I thought I was having a heart attack. I never told anyone, but I almost died at the emergency room that night. It also happened again three months after all this happened. I had to leave Virginia. What happened I am going to keep private. The next two times I went to the emergency room I thought I was having a stroke. They sent me home both time and told me to find a primary doctor. I finally found an amazing doctor. It had been a long time since I had found a primary doctor that I liked. She is amazing. To stay and have quality time with my mother, I chose to be put on an anxiety medicine and an antidepressant for one month. I knew I could not stay because of Roxy. I embraced it. I took my mother from a fragile state to a healthy state. My mother started gaining weight and looking better. She was really upset about not being able to drive anymore. I took her anywhere she wanted to go. She went from only a few calls on her birthday to everyone calling to wish her a happy birthday. I was able to get everyone to come over for her birthday weekend. It was such a good feeling to see how happy she was. My mother thanked me after that weekend was over. She told me that was her best birthday she had since my father past six years prior. No one will be able to take that from my mother and me. Not even Roxy.

On March 27, 2020, I was alone sightseeing at Desoto Park, Alabama. It was beautiful. The wat-

erfalls were breathtaking. The stay-at-home order was issued for North Carolina. I had detached
from the world to gain some inner peace. I had
stop watching the news and did not know what
was going on until the following day.

On March 28, I overheard someone at the store
talking about a stay-at-home order. I asked them
what is a stay-at-home order. They explained and
then I had to go on the internet and do some research about what was going on. I started getting
nervous about not being home with my mother
and son. I was scared that I wasn't closer and
headed home. On my way home, Roxy called and
told me I was not allowed to come home because
my mother is eighty-three and had the coronavirus. Please take note Roxy doesn't live there.
Roxy is not allowed over to my mother's house
because she steals sentimental things from my
mother. I live at my mothers with my teenage son,
Charles. Roxy went on to tell me I could not wash
clothes or take a shower there either. I told her
that is my home. I have nowhere else to go. I am
high risk also. I have metastatic breast cancer and
I had been in the woods by myself. When I was
around people, I always wore a gloves, mask and
glasses to cover my eyes, so I knew I was safe from
the coronavirus. My son Charles said that they

were suggesting that I take a shower and wash my clothes at a truck stop. I started pan-icking. I called my doctors to get a test done. I told them where I was, and they told me I should be fine to go home with my mother and son. My mother and I have the same primary doctor, so they know us both. My doctor said I did not need a coronavirus test. They said since I was in the woods and not around anyone, my mother and me would be fine.

On March 29, I arrived home and setup a tent in the woods by mother's house. I also setup a TV and a couple of heaters in the garage and was chillin'. I didn't want to upset my mother, so I just did what would not cause conflict with Roxy. If you don't listen to Roxy; she gets mad and will try to destroy you. I am not worried about me I am worried about my mother. I don't want Roxy to upset or hurt my mother. I went from the tent to the garage for four days just to be safe. Roxy is doing everything she can to get me out of that house. Roxy is jealous of my relationship with my mother.

Mom came outside giving me food and a warm blanket on April 1. I finally fell asleep. I woke up crying so hard. I called my mother and said with tears rolling down my face "Mom, can I take a shower because I hurt so bad from my cancer?"

She says, "Yes darling." I took a quick shower and rested on my bed crying. The phone rings repeatedly until my mother answered. Whatever Roxy said made my mom really upset. You could hear it in her voice then she hang up. My mother was being coached by Roxy. It is not my mother; it is Roxy. After that phone call, mom's attitude changed toward me to angry. She came to my door and started yelling at me. All I could do was say, "What did I do, why are you so angry with me?" Tears down my cheeks because I knew it wasn't my mother it was Roxy. When people are weak, that is when Roxy strikes. When someone is vulnerable, she strikes. Roxy preys on the weak. I am not the only person she has done this to. I am just hoping to be the last. Over the last six months of living with my mother, my mother said to me, "Roxy scares me. I am really scared of Roxy." On three different occasions. I remember that and don't take it lightly.

Then my son Charles came out yelling at me and blaming me for making grandmother upset. I yelled, "Leave me alone!" and shut my door. I knew what was happening and needed to stay focused. I tried to stay focused, but I couldn't. All of a sudden, I see lights flashing before my eyes. I hear loud noises in my head. They won't stop. The paramedics arrive with sirens blaring. Roxy called the paramedics on me. The paramedics called me out to the main room to get my temperature. I had no fever, and the EMS told my mother and Charles they didn't see anything wrong with me being in the house and we should all stay in our rooms. She has a 4,000 sq. ft home. We are all away from each other. My son Charles took his cat away from me; that was very upsetting to me. He removed all his things from the bathroom we shared and put them in my mother's bathroom. Everyone goes to their room. I knew Roxy wasn't done. This wasn't going to end well with me and Roxy.

On April 2, Charles comes to my door and asks if he can go with grandma to Roxy's lake house because there is no one else to watch her and help her. I said yes. I must ride this out. I must stay calm and focused.

Roxy told me she would have Charles back in two weeks on April 14.

April 4, I woke up crying about missing my son and mother. I had to lie about being sick so I could get a coronavirus test. That way they can come home at least I. Roxy had no plans of them return-ing or bringing my son back. I was tested for the flu and coronavirus.

April 7, the nurse calls I am negative for flu and

coronavirus. I told Roxy. My son was never brought back to me. I guess she had other plans with him.

April 14, I call Roxy but no one answers. I need to know where my son is. I need to talk to him. I was trying to avoid getting the police involved. I just do not want the drama. No one would answer. Then Charles texts me he's at a friend house and he is staying until the stay at home order is lifted. Where and who? I needed the address and phone number. No response. No communication. I told him I was picking him up tomorrow and all we must do was communicate and the police would not be involved. Roxy has had my mother and Charles isolated away from the entire family for two weeks. I am getting worried.

April 15, I went to look at places to rent. Charles and I had a heart to heart before we moved there. I told him, I don't know what is going to happen. I have put some funds in a local bank where we moved from. I would have to drive twelve hours and go into the bank to access the funds. It is not a lot, but it is enough in case anything goes wrong. I am hoping for the best, but I do feel it will not end well. Things almost never go the positive way I want them to go. I told him that I wanted him to stay and protect his grandmother from Roxy if anything happens to me. He agreed. I also told him that I don't want him to tell anyone about this conversation because I don't know who has been compromised. He agreed. At that point, me and my son don't even need to talk. We both know what Roxy is doing.

That morning, I left early and went to an apartment complex by a college. Due to the coronavirus, I couldn't even turn in an application. They said I couldn't even do a walk through because of the stay-at-home order. Roxy got me in a really bad situation. I can handle anything she throws my way to protect my mother. I was not prepared for COVID-19, so I embrace it and move forward. A 2bed/1bath house. A lady with her son rode by in her wheelchair and told me I didn't want to live there because there was just a shooting the night prior. I told her thank you and have a blessed day. I headed to a 2bed/1bath mobile home. It was nice but not available right away. I went to the store to get my mother's favorite candy bar and my son's favorite drink and chips. I went by Roxy's lake house where she had kidnapped and was holding my mother and son hostage. I need to have communication with my son to let him know what we feared was happening. This way he would be prepared. I parked in Roxy's driveway and went to talk to my son through the window downstairs. I knew something wasn't right I could feel it. I knew things weren't going to end well. I also knew it might be the last time I see my son. That is not what I want it is just reality. No one is talking to me, and Roxy has kidnapped my son and are refusing to give him back. I also wanted to tell him I was sorry for not listening to him about being homeschooled. I was willing to try it with him. He comes to the window and says, "Roxy said get off the property or you will be arrested." I said I will call them because you need to come with me. This isn't right. I call the police, and they come out. Roxy shows up, gives the sheriff the restraining orders and I can't take my son. I must leave my mother's house and have nowhere to go. I slept in my car, and the pain was unbearable. All I could do is drive, cry and pray to my higher power. I did not go to the court date. The judge said I was not served properly continued it until May 22nd @ 9 a.m. Yes, I knew they weren't signed by a judge. I also knew that the sheriff should have brought me my son and didn't. This doesn't upset me. Thank you, Sherriff's Office, for not bringing me my son, even though it hurts me to the bone. I know my son (my soldier) is in place to protect my mother from Roxy. I know my mother will be safe with him there.

I am worried if my mother gets sick, she won't be able to get to a court date to have it removed. If I get sick and pass that would mess my son up more than anyone could fathom. It is out of character for both to do this. Violence is out of character for me. I know it's Roxy. It says firearms on this illegal restraining order. I have never owned a gun. It is my right to own one if I chose. I have chosen not to own a firearm because of what happened with Kyle. I am no way against guns. Roxy cannot take my rights away. I am just tired of being made out to be someone I am not.

When this happened, the thoughts going through my head were of disbelief because in forty-seven years I have never been evicted. I have had full custody of all three of my children their entire life. Sarah, my daughter, thirty, is a project manager. Ryan, my son, twenty-five is a Marine. Charles, sixteen, he is my baby, so he gets a lot the other two did not, not because I love him more it is due to my having more money than I did before. He gets a cell phone and name brand shoes the others never received from me. Charles is a deep thinker like me. I had never had a child taken from me like Roxy took Charles. It had trauma-tized me. I have never had a restraining order served to me. I will always walk away. I am not a violent person. If someone attacks me, I will have no other chose but to fight back. I walk around with love; I don't like to fight. My entire life, I have never been to jail or prison. Roxy has declared psychological warfare on me. Roxy, abort your mission of hate. You have underestimated your target (me) You have picked the wrong target. Your battle is not with me it is from within you.

This was the first time in thirty years I have lived by myself with no child. As a matter of fact, this the first time I have ever lived by myself in forty-seven years. All of this is devastating to me. I cry so hard and the pain is so great that my heart physically hurts.

The thoughts running through my mind were as follows.

My mom is eighty-three, Charles my son, I have metastatic breast cancer, and if these orders went through if any of us got sick or even died, we could not see each other. What do I want? I want both restraining orders dropped there is no evidence to support their claim. The eighth date of the alleged incident we didn't even see each other. Roxy had them isolated at the lake house from April 2 to past the 15th when I was wrongly evicted. I was not served properly. There are no marks, pictures, no police report. I have my test results for the coronavirus that are negative. I have his best friend's mother writing a character reference letter for me. We have known each other since the boys were in seventh grade. I can get his elementary and middle school records and attendance from where he grew up. He had perfect attendance and was on the honor roll. I had bought a house or a new car so Charles had whatever he wanted. His life was not bad like he is saying in a text; in fact, I can tell Roxy wrote for him. Roxy has kidnapped my son and mother and interrogated them until they caved. The only way for it to stop is if they both sign. Roxy is holding them hostage until they sign. Oh my, they have broken my heart and soul, and they do not care. I want my son back my rights were never taken away. I didn't do anything to justify this. That is everything I was thinking. What I want and what happens are to different things.

Roxy began bullying me again. This was the third time Roxy has done this to me throughout my lifetime. It must be the last or I will die, I tell myself. I am as good as dead if I don't stop her mission of hate. Roxy has bad mouthed my parenting to my son for eight months to him. Roxy has criticized me every day for eight months now.

Damned if I do, damned if I don't. Roxy constantly undermined me. My son has got to get away from Roxy; he is losing respect for me, and I will lose him to parental alienation. It is a toxic environment for us both. Roxy is trying to do something with him I don't know what. I need to push it all out of my head and remember that first conversation prior to moving in and hope he remembers. Love always wins in the end. Some way somehow it just does. I do not know how much damage Roxy has done to our relationship because I can't talk to him. My heart physically hurts, and I cannot stop crying. It is my mother. No, don't take my mother from me. Roxy can call her, and I can't. Roxy is evil and poison.

You know, things are not always as they appear. I have just escaped the toxic hold Roxy has had on me. I looked around and all I saw were people that had been compromised. Someone said, "Only you can change that." It all hit me like a ton of bricks. If I don't take drastic measures to end Roxy's mission of hate, I will pay dearly. How will I pay, you might ask? I will pay with my happiness. Roxy keeps trying to get me to live in the same state as her. I know I have clearly stated my entire life I don't want to live there. Roxy wants me right by her so she can take care of me.

I don't need anyone to take care of me, so I don't understand. I never asked for help from anyone so that makes it hard to understand why. Being a deep thinker like I am, it is crucial for me to detach from everyone and be alone. It is the only way I survive in this world. National parks or any sort of nature is where I can relax, and it always brings me peace. It feels like Roxy wants to set me up like I am dying just because I have metastatic breast cancer. I am not dying I am living so what is there problem. I love to live life on the edge, meet new people, go and see things I haven't seen before. Stop treating me like I am dying because I am not dying, I am living. I could never just sit in a house and do the same thing every day. Over these few months I have realized I will have to let everyone go in order to be happy. I can never let anyone back in because my happiness is not worth the sacrifice. I have too much to lose which is my happiness. It is heartbreaking that it has come to this point. Why can't they understand that letting go of someone is not always a negative thing? Sometimes you need to let someone go not so they will fall. You need to let them go so they can fly. If you don't, they will eventually cut you out of there life forever, then you will never see or hear from them again. My children are my world. They are what motivates me to be a better person.

What did I do after all this happened, you might ask? Sometimes you must take two steps backwards to go forward. I detached myself from everyone and everything to gain a new perspective. I was not going to allow them to win, so I needed to turn it around in my thinking. I always have been able to pull out a positive reason in a negative situation my entire life. This situation took much longer. I came up with a message to my mother: "I am the woman I am today because of you. Thank you for trying to protect me from Roxy. Because you were willing to let me go, I can now spread my wings and fly. I will do amazing things mother, just watch. I will succeed. I love you, Your baby girl." I then posted a picture and said to my son, "I keep heading west bound. You wouldn't happen to know why? lol." I did this because his cat is named West, and every time, I heard the GPS say "west," it felt good, and I would smile. I am happy from within. I can look myself in the mirror and know I am a good person no matter what anyone says. It is the best feeling in the world. I love me.

I foresee my three adult children paying for my bad decision of allowing Roxy back in my life if I do not do something drastic. I am powerless. For me to move forward, to be able to look myself in the mirror, and be happy with myself, I have to know I did everything I could to stop Roxy from steeling from my children when I pass. This has traumatized my mother and me.

I love Roxy so much but because she was not willing to let me go so I could fly I have no other choice but to let her go. Roxy abort your mission of hate with me. You have picked the wrong target. Your battle is not with me it is within yourself. Roxy is like a leach, sucking the life right out of me. So, in my eyes she is trying to kill me because she has stopped me from growing. Do you know you can kill someone by not letting them go? You are happy while you are holding onto them, but they are dying inside. You are slowly suffocating them by not letting them be who they really are, by not letting them do the things they are passionate about. Sometimes people don't need to change, they just need to change who they have around them. When you meet someone, you should accept them for who they are not looking at things you want to change. We all must stay true to ourselves. For me to survive in this world, I never will allow Roxy back into my life. If I do, I will die. I don't have time for this. I had to mourn all of my family's death just to stay alive because of Roxy. This is hard for me to do. I have cried for months. It was the worst pain I have felt in my entire life. I had to change my number and get my thoughts together. I listened repeatedly to motivational videos. I did not realize how much they helped until later. I got down on my hands and knees and prayed to my higher power. I begged for my pain not to be in vain, I begged for my three adult children wouldn't pay for my mistakes of allowing Roxy back in my life. I prayed for my purpose. It wasn't until four months later that I prayed again because the pain was unbearable for my purpose. I saw several visions and stop crying. My visions are only for my knowledge. I have learned if you tell the wrong person your dreams or plan for a better life, they will smash them. It is called sabotage because of the hate in their heart.

Roxy wants me to be just like her because she is socially accepted. I would never want to be like her not because she is socially accepted but because of all the hate in her heart. I would much rather be me with love and good intentions in my heart. When someone with hate in their heart does mean things, you might get hurt but, in the end, they continue with hate. When you continue with hate it only hurt no one else but you in the end. You were unhappy that whole time and, in the end, you are still unhappy. If you have love in your heart you will get hurt but it shows you who is toxic. When your heart is full of love, in the end you feel like you have more knowledge, strength and yes, even more love. It is the best feeling in the world to have survived and still have a heart full of love. It is a process and as you can see it has been a lifetime. I wouldn't trade it for anything. I love my life just the way it is.

I am living in my car at truck stops because of Roxy, and I am perfectly fine with that. From the outside it might look like I am miserable. After writing this book I feel happiness I have never felt before. I know my two sons are there to protect my mother from Roxy. Both of my sons are soldiers.

One night I was tossing and turning and could not sleep. I could feel that my mother was worried. I told my mother in a message online. "Mother don't worry it will be ok. I have both my adult sons there to protect you. They are both soldiers, mother. I will see you at your house September 28, 2021. On September 29, 2021, my mission will be completed. I love you mother, and miss you a lot. – Your baby girl" That is at least my dream. My dream is to let go of Kyle on his birthday, September 28, 2021. Since my mother and I could not be together for her eighty-fourth birthday because of Roxy. My dream is to be with my mother September 29, 2021, for her eighty-fifth birthday. I am going to sleep in my car until then because I have been displaced from my home by Roxy. I am staying at different truck stops until then. I just must let you know, if one more trucker asks me to meet them in their truck, I am going to scream and walk away. Please know it is not you it is me. I don't get paid for sex, and I never have. I do take it as a compliment. I just cannot take anymore judgment. At one point of my life, if I had the self-confidence, I would have been a stripper. I lack the self-confidence that strippers have. So, I admire them and had to find something else to do with my life. To me I need to have a mental connection with someone before I do anything. I love passionate sex just not with anyone. I love intense passion. Sex without passion is just sex. If I don't have someone in my life, I am passionate about, I just refrain from sex. No big deal.

Roxy says I am a bad mother because of the music I listen to. In life, you pick your battles. I have made my online account public and posted some of the music I listen to. You know why I did this? I did this because your battle is not with me it is with the various artists that sing/write those songs. It cannot be just one song it has to be all of them. You have just picked a battle with all of them. I love all kinds of music. This also gives my son the tools to survive in this world without drugs or alcohol. He is a deep thinker just like me. We are different, but what makes us different makes us beautiful.

After all of this happened, there were so many things I could have done. There are so many other things I could have spent my money on. What I decided to do is embrace it. Roll with the punches with a heart full of love and a smile on my face. I am displaced from my home and live in my car. I bought a laptop and wrote a book about how wonderful my mother has been to me my entire life. I will mail her the first copy to read. I know Roxy could put a warrant out for my arrest against my mother's will for giving her a copy of my book. If that happens, and I go to jail, I will do it will a smile on my face because love always wins in the end. It might not look like it from the outside but from the inside love won with me and my mother. If you ever feel alone and like no one understands you, please know I do. You have the power to change the ending of anything bad in life even total devastation by telling your story or writing a book. I lived on a healthy life and never died from breast cancer at least that is my dream.

Now I can let go of everything that has happened in my past. I am moving forward in life with a smile on my face, love in my heart and good intentions. Thank you for listening to me. I appreciate you.

Due to unforeseen circumstances, I have been displaced from where I reside with my mother and son due to the COVID-19. I am displaced in my vehicle until I can be with my mother and son again.

I now wear a black mask that says "LOVE" on it. Do you know why I do this? It is not because I understand or know the struggles some encounter day to day. It is because when I told my granddaughter that she could be the first women president if she wanted to. I want to make sure she feels that she has the same opportunities that I felt like I had growing up.

ABOUT THE AUTHOR

TARA HERRING graduated from TESST College of Technology in Virginia and George C. Marshall High School in Falls Church, Virginia. She hopes sharing her story will help at least one person not feel alone and will give them hope. She also wants to give her mother the positive credit that she deserves for being a loving mother. This is Tara's first book. Learn more about her and this book at *www.facebook.com/LuvAlwaysWins2021*.

www.ingramcontent.com/pod-product-compliance
Lightning Source LLC
Chambersburg PA
CBHW061200040426

42445CB00013B/1753